AF216404

Impressum
Verlag: BABADADA GmbH, Nedderfeld 112 , 22529 Hamburg
Geschäftsführer / Verlagsleitung: Harald Hof
Druck: Books on Demand GmbH, In de Tarpen 42, 22848 Norderstedt

Imprint
Publisher: BABADADA GmbH, Nedderfeld 112 , 22529 Hamburg, Germany
Managing Director / Publishing direction: Harald Hof
Print: Books on Demand GmbH, In de Tarpen 42, 22848 Norderstedt

classroom
salón de clases

divide
dividir

186/2

board
pizarrón

school yard
patio

teacher
maestro

paper
pap

write
escribir

pen
bolígrafo

desk
escritorio

ruler
regla

book
libro

pupil
alumno

satchel

mochila

pencil case

caja de lápices

pencil

lápiz

pencil sharpener

sacapuntas

rubber

goma de borrar

drawing pad

bloc de dibujo

drawing

dibujo

paintbrush

pincel

paint box

caja de lápices de color

scissors

tijeras

glue

pegamento

exercise book

libro de ejercicios

homework

tarea

number

número

add

sumar

subtract

restar

multiply

multiplicar

calculate

calcular

letter

letra

alphabet

alfabeto

word

palabra

text

texto

read

leer

chalk

tiza

lesson

lección

register

cuaderno de clase

exam

examen

certificate

certificado

school uniform

uniforme

education

educación

encyclopedia

enciclopedia

university

universidad

microscope

microscopio

map

mapa

waste-paper basket

bote de basura

hotel
hotel

hostel
hostel

bureau de change
casa de cambio

car
carro

language
idioma

yes / no
sí / no

Okay
Órale

hello
hola

translator
traductor

Thank you
Gracias

how much is…?

¿cuánto cuesta…?

I do not understand

No entiendo

problem

problema

Good evening!

¡Buenas tardes!

Good morning!

¡Buenos días!

Good night!

¡Buenas noches!

bye bye

adiós

direction

dirección

luggage

equipaje

bag

bolsa

backpack

mochila

guest

invitado

room

recámara

sleeping bag

bolsa de dormir

tent

tienda de campaña

tourist information

información turística

beach

playa

credit card

tarjeta de crédito

breakfast

desayuno

lunch

almuerzo

dinner

cena

ticket

billete

lift

ascensor

stamp

sello

border

frontera

customs

aduana

embassy

embajada

visa

visa

passport

pasaporte

aeroplane
avión

ship
barco

fire engine
camión de bomberos

bus
autobús

truck
camión

motorboat
lancha a motor

bike
bicicleta

car
carro

ferry

ferry

boat

bote

motorbike

motocicleta

police car

patrulla

racing car

coche de carreras

rental car

auto para rentar

car sharing

renta de autos

breakdown truck

grúa

refuse truck

camión recolector de basura

motor

motor

fuel

gasolina

petrol station

gasolinera

traffic sign

señal de tráfico

traffic

tránsito

traffic jam

embotellamiento

car park

aparcamiento

train station

estación de tren

tracks

vías

train

tren

tram

tranvía

carriage

vagón

helicopter

helicóptero

airport

aeropuerto

tower

torre

passenger

pasajero

container

contenedor

carton

caja de cartón

cart

carretilla

basket

cesta

take off / land

despegar / aterrizar

city
ciudad

village

pueblo

city centre

centro de ciudad

house

casa

cinema
cine

advert
anuncio

street lamp
farol

CINEMA

street
calle

taxi
taxi

snack shop
dulcería

pedestrian
peatón

pavement
banqueta

zebra crossing
paso peatonal

bin
bote de basura

crossing
cruce

traffic lights
semáforo

hut
....
cabaña

flat
....
apartamento

train station
....
estación de tren

town hall
....
ayuntamiento

museum
....
museo

school
....
escuela

university

universidad

bank

banco

hospital

hospital

hotel

hotel

pharmacy

farmacia

office

oficina

book shop

librería

shop

tienda

florist's

florería

supermarket

supermercado

market

mercado

department store

grandes tiendas

fishmonger's

pescadería

shopping centre

centro comercial

harbour

puerto

park

parque

bench

banco

bridge

puente

stairs

escaleras

underground

metro

tunnel

túnel

bus stop

parada de autobús

bar

bar

restaurant

restaurante

postbox

buzón

street sign

letrero

parking meter

parquímetro

zoo

zoológico

swimming pool

alberca

mosque

mezquita

farm
granja

pollution
contaminación

graveyard
cementerio

church
iglesia

playground
área de niños

temple
templo

landscape

paisaje

signpost
señal

way
camino

meadow
pradera

stone
piedra

tree
árbol

hiker
caminante

river
río

grass
pasto

flower
flor

valley

valle

hill

montaña

lake

lago

forest

bosque

desert

desierto

volcano

volcán

castle

castillo

rainbow

arco iris

mushroom

champiñón

palm tree

palmera

mosquito

mosquito

fly

mosca

ant

hormiga

bee

abeja

spider

araña

landscape - paisaje

beetle

escarabajo

frog

rana

squirrel

ardilla

hedgehog

erizo

hare

liebre

owl

lechuza

bird

pájaro

swan

cisne

boar

jabalí

deer

ciervo

moose

alce

dam

embalse

wind turbine

turbina eólica

solar panel

pansolar

climate

clima

waiter
camarero

menu
menú

chair
silla

pizza
pizza

soup
sopa

tablecloth
mantel

cutlery
cubiertos

starter

entrada

main course

plato fuerte

dessert

postre

drinks

bebidas

food

comida

bottle

botella

fast food

comida rápida

street food

comida de calle

teapot

tetera

sugar bowl

azucarera

portion

porción

espresso machine

cafetera espresso

high chair

periquera

bill

cuenta

tray

charola

knife

cuchillo

fork

tenedor

spoon

cuchara

teaspoon

cuchara de té

serviette

servilleta

glass

vaso

restaurant - restaurante

plate

plato

soup plate

plato hondo

saucer

plato

sauce

salsa

salt pot

salero

pepper mill

molino para pimienta

vinegar

vinagre

oil

aceite

spices

especias

ketchup

kétchup

mustard

mostaza

mayonnaise

mayonesa

special offer
oferta especial

customer
cliente

FOR

dairy
productos lácteos

fruit
fruta

trolley
carrito para compras

butcher's
carnicería

baker's
panadería

weigh
pesar

vegetables
vegetales

meat
carne

frozen food
alimentos congelados

cold meat

carnes frías

tinned food

alimentos enlatados

washing powder

detergente en polvo

sweets

dulces

household products

electrodomésticos

cleaning products

productos de limpieza

salesperson

vendedora

till

caja

cashier

cajero

shopping list

lista de compras

opening hours

horario de atención al público

wallet

cartera

credit card

tarjeta de crédito

bag

bolsa

plastic bag

bolsa de plástico

water

agua

juice

jugo

milk

leche

coke

refresco de cola

wine

vino

beer

cerveza

alcohol

alcohol

cocoa

cacao

tea

té

coffee

café

espresso

espresso

cappuccino

cappuccino

banana

plátano

apple

manzana

orange

naranja

melon

melón

lemon

limón

carrot

zanahoria

garlic

ajo

bamboo

bambú

onion

cebolla

mushroom

champiñón

nuts

nueces

noodles

fideos

spaghetti

espaguetis

rice

arroz

salad

ensalada

chips

patatas fritas

fried potatoes

patatas fritas

pizza

pizza

hamburger

hamburguesa

sandwich

emparedado

cutlet

filete

ham

jamón

salami

salami

sausage

salchicha

chicken

pollo

roast

asado

fish

pescado

porridge oats

copos de avena

muesli

muesli

cornflakes

copos de maíz

flour

harina

croissant

cuernito

bread roll

bolillo

bread

pan

toast

tostada

biscuits

galletas

butter

mantequilla

curd

cuajada

cake

pastel

egg

huevo

fried egg

huevo frito

cheese

queso

ice cream

helado

sugar

azúcar

honey

miel

jam

mermelada

chocolate spread

crema de chocolate

curry

curry

goat

cabra

cow

vaca

calf

ternero

pig

cerdo

piglet

lechón

bull

toro

farm - granja

goose

ganso

duck

pato

chick

pollo

hen

gallina

cock

gallo

rat

rata

cat

gato

mouse

ratón

ox

buey

dog

perro

doghouse

casa dperro

garden hose

manguera

watering can

regadera

scythe

guadaña

plough

arado

sickle

hoz

hoe

azadón

pitchfork

horquilla

axe

hacha

wheelbarrow

carretilla

trough

bebedero

milk can

bote de leche

sack

saco

fence

valla

stable

establo

greenhouse

invernadero

soil

suelo

seed

semilla

fertilizer

fertilizador

combine harvester

cosechadora

harvest

cosechar

harvest

cosecha

yams

camote

wheat

trigo

soy

soja

potato

patata

corn

maíz

rapeseed

semilde colza

fruit tree

árbol frutal

cassava

mandioca

cereals

cereales

living room

estancia

bathroom

baño

kitchen

cocina

bedroom

recámara

child's room

recámara de los niños

dining room

comedor

floor

suelo

wall

pared

ceiling

techo

cellar

sótano

sauna

sauna

balcony

balcón

terrace

terraza

pool

alberca

lawn mower

cortacésped

sheet

sábana

bedspread

colcha

bed

cama

broom

escoba

bucket

balde

switch

interruptor

carpet

alfombra

curtain

cortina

table

mesa

chair

silla

rocking chair

mecedora

armchair

sillón

book

libro

blanket

frazada

decoration

decoración

firewood

leña

film

película

hi-fi equipment

equipo de música

key

llave

newspaper

periódico

painting

pintura

poster

póster

radio

radio

notepad

cuaderno

hoover

aspiradora

cactus

cactus

candle

vela

fridge
refrigerador

microwave oven
microondas

kitchen scales
báscude cocina

toaster
tostadora

detergent
detergente

oven
horno

freezer
congelador

dishwasher
lavavajillas

cooker
opresión

pot
olla

cast-iron pot
olde hierro fundido

wok / kadai
wok

pan
sartén

kettle
hervidor

steamer

vaporera

baking tray

charode horno

crockery

loza

mug

taza

bowl

bol

chopsticks

palillos

ladle

cucharón

spatula

espátula

whisk

batidora

strainer

colador

sieve

colador

grater

rallador

mortar

mortero

barbecue

barbacoa

open fire

fogata

chopping board

tabpara picar

rolling pin

rodillo para amasar

corkscrew

sacacorchos

can

lata

can opener

abrelatas

pot holder

guante de cocina

sink

fregadero

brush

cepillo

sponge

esponja

blender

batidora

deep freezer

congelador

baby bottle

biberón

tap

llave

heating
calefacción

shower
ducha

towel
toalla

shower curtain
cortina de ducha

bubble bath
baño de espuma

bathtub
tina

glass
vaso

washing machine
lavadora

tap
llave

tiles
baldosas

potty
bacinica

sink
fregadero

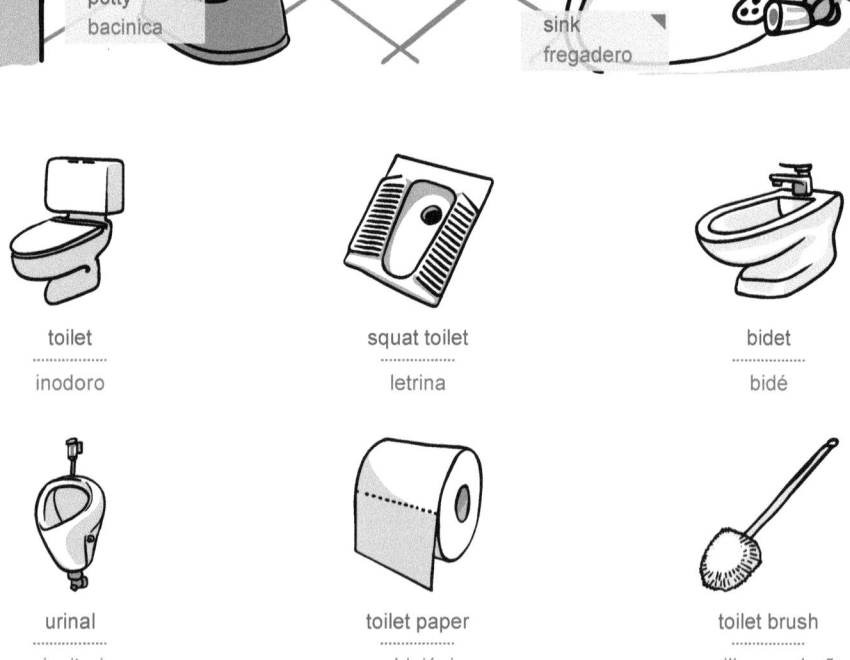

toilet	squat toilet	bidet
inodoro	letrina	bidé
urinal	toilet paper	toilet brush
mingitorio	paphigiénico	cepillo para baño

toothbrush

cepillo de dientes

toothpaste

pasta dental

dental floss

hilo dental

wash

lavar

handheld shower

ducha de mano

douche

ducha vaginal

basin

fregadero

back brush

cepillo de espalda

soap

jabón

shower gel

gde ducha

shampoo

champú

flannel

toallita

drain

drenaje

cream

crema

deodorant

desodorante

mirror

espejo

hand mirror

espejo de tocador

razor

máquina para afeitar

shaving foam

espuma de afeitar

aftershave

loción para después de afeitar

comb

peine

brush

cepillo

hair dryer

secadora

hairspray

laca

makeup

maquillaje

lipstick

lápiz labial

nail varnish

esmalte para uñas

cotton wool

algodón

nail scissors

tijeras para uñas

perfume

perfume

washbag

estuche para cosméticos

stool

taburete

weighing scale

báscula

bathrobe

bata

rubber gloves

guantes de goma

tampon

tampón

sanitary towel

toalsanitaria

chemical toilet

baño móvil

alarm clock
despertador

cuddly toy
peluche

toy car
carro de juguete

rattle
sonaja

doll's house
casa de muñecas

present
regalo

balloon

globo

bed

cama

pram

carriola

deck of cards

cartas

jigsaw

rompecabezas

comic

cómic

lego bricks

piezas de lego

building blocks

bloques para jugar

action figure

figura de acción

babygrow

mameluco

frisbee

frisbee

mobile

móvil para bebés

board game

juego de mesa

dice

dados

model train set

tren eléctrico

dummy

maniquí

party

fiesta

picture book

álbum de fotos

ball

balón

doll

muñeca

play

jugar

sandpit

arenero

swing

columpio

toys

juguetes

video game console

consode videojuegos

tricycle

triciclo

teddy bear

oso de peluche

wardrobe

clóset

clothing

ropa

socks

calcetines

stockings

pantimedias

tights

mallas

scarf
bufanda

umbrella
paraguas

t-shirt
playera

belt
cinto

boots
botas

slippers
chanclas

trainers
tenis

sandals
....
sandalias

shoes
....
zapatos

rubber boots
....
botas de goma

underpants
....
ropa interior

bra
....
brasier

vest
....
chaleco

body

body

trousers

pantalones

jeans

pantalones de mezclilla

skirt

falda

blouse

blusa

shirt

camisa

pullover

suéter

hoodie

sudadera

blazer

saco sport

jacket

chamarra

coat

abrigo

raincoat

impermeable

costume

traje

dress

vestido

wedding dress

vestido de novia

suit

traje

nightgown

camisón

pyjamas

pijama

sari

sari

headscarf

pañuelo para cabeza

turban

turbante

burqa

burka

kaftan

caftán

abaya

abaya

swimsuit

traje de baño

trunks

short de baño

shorts

shorts

tracksuit

pants

apron

delantal

gloves

guantes

button

botón

glasses

gafas

bracelet

brazalete

necklace

collar

ring

anillo

earring

arete

cap

gorra

coat hanger

gancho

hat

sombrero

tie

corbata

zip

cierre

helmet

casco

braces

tirantes

school uniform

uniforme

uniform

uniforme

bib
babero

dummy
maniquí

nappy
pañal

office
oficina

server
servidor

filing cabinet
archivo

printer
impresora

monitor
monitor

paper
pap

mouse
mouse

desk
escritorio

folder
carpeta

keyboard
teclado

chair
silla

waste-paper basket
bote de basura

computer
computadora

coffee mug
taza de café

calculator
calculadora

internet
internet

laptop
notebook

letter
carta

message
mensaje

mobile
móvil

network
red

photocopier
fotocopiadora

software
software

telephone
teléfono

plug socket
tomacorriente

fax machine
fax

form
formulario

document
documento

buy

comprar

pay

pagar

trade

hacer negocios

money

dinero

 USD

dollar

dólar

 EUR

euro

euro

 JPY

yen

yen

 RUB

rouble

rublo

 CHF

Swiss franc

franco suizo

 CNY

renminbi yuan

yuan

 INR

rupee

rupia

cashpoint

cajero automático

bureau de change

casa de cambio

gold

oro

silver

plata

oil

petróleo

energy

energía

price

precio

contract

contrato

tax

impuesto

stock

acción

work

trabajar

employee

empleado

employer

empleador

factory

fábrica

shop

tienda

police officer
policía

fireman
bombero

pilot
piloto

cook
cocinero

doctor
médico

gardener
jardinero

carpenter
carpintero

seamstress
costurera

judge
juez

chemist
farmacéutico

actor
actor

bus driver

conductor de autobús

taxi driver

taxista

fisherman

pescador

cleaning lady

señora de limpieza

roofer

instalador de techos

waiter

camarero

hunter

cazador

painter

pintor

baker

panadero

electrician

electricista

builder

obrero

engineer

ingeniero

butcher

carnicero

plumber

plomero

postman

cartero

soldier

soldado

architect

arquitecto

cashier

cajero

florist

florista

hairdresser

peluquero

conductor

cobrador

mechanic

mecánico

captain

capitán

dentist

dentista

scientist

científico

rabbi

rabino

imam

imán

monk

monje

clergyman

sacerdote

hammer
martillo

pliers
pinza

screwdriver
desarmador

spanner
llave

torch
linterna

digger
excavadora

toolbox
caja de herramientas

ladder
escalera de mano

saw
sierra

nails
clavos

drill
taladro

repair
reparar

shovel
pala

Damn!
¡Maldición!

dustpan
recogedor

paint pot
bote de pintura

screws
tornillos

musical instruments
instrumentos musicales

loudspeaker
altavoz

drum kit
batería

double bass
contrabajo

trumpet
trompeta

guitar
guitarra

piano

piano

violin

violín

bass

bajo

timpani

timbales

drums

tambor

keyboard

teclado

saxophone

saxofón

flute

flauta

microphone

micrófono

entrance
entrada

tiger
tigre

cage
jaula

zebra
cebra

animal feed
alimento para animales

panda
oso panda

animals
animales

elephant
elefante

kangaroo
canguro

rhino
rinoceronte

gorilla
gorila

bear
oso

camel

camello

ostrich

avestruz

lion

león

monkey

mono

flamingo

flamenco

parrot

loro

polar bear

oso polar

penguin

pingüino

shark

tiburón

peacock

pavo real

snake

serpiente

crocodile

cocodrilo

zookeeper

guardián de zoológico

seal

foca

jaguar

jaguar

pony

poni

leopard

leopardo

hippo

hipopótamo

giraffe

jirafa

eagle

águila

boar

jabalí

fish

pescado

turtle

tortuga

walrus

morsa

fox

zorro

gazelle

gacela

American football
fútbol americano

cycling
ciclismo

tennis
tenis

basketball
baloncesto

swimming
natación

boxing
boxeo

ice hockey
hockey sobre hielo

football
fútbol

badminton
bádminton

athletics
atletismo

handball
handball

skiing
esquí

polo
polo

jump
saltar

laugh
reír

hug
abrazar

walk
caminar

sing
cantar

dream
soñar

pray
rezar

kiss
besar

write
escribir

draw
dibujar

show
mostrar

push
empujar

give
dar

take
tomar

have
tener

do
hacer

be
ser

stand
estar parado

run
correr

pull
jalar

throw
arrojar

fall
caer

lie
estar acostado

wait
esperar

carry
llevar

sit
estar sentado

get dressed
vestirse

sleep
dormir

wake up
despertar

look at

mirar

cry

llorar

stroke

acariciar

comb

peinar

talk

hablar

understand

entender

ask

preguntar

listen

escuchar

drink

beber

eat

comer

tidy up

ordenar

love

amar

cook

cocinar

drive

conducir

fly

volar

activities - actividades

sail

navegar

calculate

calcular

read

leer

learn

aprender

work

trabajar

marry

casarse

sew

coser

brush teeth

cepillarse los dientes

kill

matar

smoke

fumar

send

enviar

grandmother
abuela

grandfather
abuelo

father
padre

mother
madre

baby
bebé

daughter
hija

son
hijo

guest

invitado

aunt

tía

uncle

tío

brother

hermano

sister

hermana

forehead
frente

eye
ojo

shoulder
hombro

finger
dedo

face
cara

chin
barbilla

hand
mano

breast
pecho

leg
pierna

arm
brazo

baby

bebé

man

hombre

woman

mujer

girl

niña

boy

niño

head

cabeza

back

espalda

belly

barriga

belly button

ombligo

toe

dedo dpie

heel

talón

bone

hueso

hip

cadera

knee

rodilla

elbow

codo

nose

nariz

bottom

pompis

skin

piel

cheek

mejilla

ear

oído

lip

labio

mouth

boca

tooth

diente

tongue

lengua

brain

cerebro

heart

corazón

muscle

músculo

lung

pulmón

liver

hígado

stomach

estómago

kidneys

riñones

sex

sexo

condom

condón

ovum

óvulo

semen

semen

pregnancy

embarazo

menstruation

menstruación

vagina

vagina

penis

pene

eyebrow

ceja

hair

cabello

neck

cuello

hospital
hospital

ambulance
ambulancia

wheelchair
silde ruedas

fracture
fractura

doctor

médico

emergency room

sade emergencias

nurse

enfermera

emergency

emergencia

unconscious

inconsciente

pain

dolor

injury

lesión

bleeding

hemorragia

heart attack

infarto

stroke

accidente cerebrovascular

allergy

alergia

cough

tos

fever

fiebre

flu

gripa

diarrhoea

diarrea

headache

dolor de cabeza

cancer

cáncer

diabetes

diabetes

surgeon

cirujano

scalpel

bisturí

operation

operación

CT
TC

x-ray
rayos x

ultrasound
ultrasonido

face mask
mascarilla

disease
enfermedad

waiting room
sade espera

crutch
muleta

plaster
vendita

bandage
vendaje

injection
inyección

stethoscope
estetoscopio

stretcher
camilla

clinical thermometer
termómetro

birth
nacimiento

overweight
sobrepeso

hearing aid

audífono

disinfectant

desinfectante

infection

infección

virus

virus

HIV / AIDS

VIH / SIDA

medicine

medicina

vaccination

vacunación

tablets

tabletas

pill

pastilanticonceptiva

emergency call

llamada de emergencia

blood pressure monitor

medidor de presión

ill / healthy

enfermo / sano

Help!

¡Socorro!

alarm

alarma

assault

agresión

attack

ataque

danger

peligro

emergency exit

salida de emergencia

Fire!

¡Fuego!

fire extinguisher

extintor de incendios

accident

accidente

first-aid kit

botiquín de primeros
auxilios

SOS

SOS

police

policía

Europe

Europa

North America

Norteamérica

South America

Sudamérica

Africa

África

Asia

Asia

Australia

Australia

Atlantic

Atlántico

Pacific

Pacífico

Indian Ocean

Océano Índico

Antarctic Ocean

Océano Antártico

Arctic Ocean

Océano Ártico

North Pole

polo norte

South Pole

polo sur

Antarctica

Antártida

Earth

tierra

land

tierra

sea

mar

island

isla

nation

nación

state

estado

clock face

esfera

hour hand

manecilde las horas

minute hand

minutero

second hand

segundero

What time is it?

¿Qué hora es?

day

día

time

hora

now

ahora

digital watch

reloj digital

minute

minuto

hour

hora

Monday
lunes

Wednesday
miércoles

Friday
viernes

Tuesday
martes

Saturday
sábado

Thursday
jueves

Sunday
domingo

yesterday
ayer

today
hoy

tomorrow
mañana

morning
mañana

noon
mediodía

evening
tarde

business days
días laborables

weekend
fin de semana

rain
lluvia

spring
primavera

summer
verano

wind
viento

autumn
otoño

snow
nieve

winter
invierno

weather forecast
....
pronóstico dtiempo

thermometer
....
termómetro

sunshine
....
sol

cloud
....
nube

fog
....
niebla

humidity
....
humedad

lightning

rayo

thunder

trueno

storm

tormenta

hail

granizo

monsoon

monzón

flood

inundación

ice

hielo

January

enero

February

febrero

March

marzo

April

abril

May

mayo

June

junio

July

julio

August

agosto

September
septiembre

October
octubre

November
noviembre

December
diciembre

shapes
formas

circle
círculo

square
cuadrado

rectangle
rectángulo

triangle
triángulo

sphere
esfera

cube
cubo

white
blanco

yellow
amarillo

orange
naranja

pink
rosa

red
rojo

purple
morado

blue
azul

green
verde

brown
marrón

grey
gris

black
negro

a lot / a little

mucho / poco

angry / calm

enojado / tranquilo

beautiful / ugly

bonito / feo

beginning / end

principio / fin

big / small

grande / pequeño

bright / dark

claro / oscuro

brother / sister

hermano / hermana

clean / dirty

limpio / sucio

complete / incomplete

completo / incompleto

day / night

día / noche

dead / alive

muerto / vivo

wide / narrow

ancho / angosto

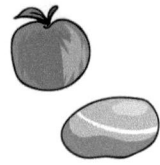

edible / inedible

comestible / no comestible

evil / kind

malo / amable

excited / bored

entusiasmado / aburrido

fat / thin

gordo / delgado

first / last

primero / último

friend / enemy

amigo / enemigo

full / empty

lleno / vacío

hard / soft

duro / blando

heavy / light

pesado / ligero

hunger / thirst

hambre / sed

ill / healthy

enfermo / sano

illegal / legal

ilegal / legal

intelligent / stupid

inteligente / tonto

left / right

izquierda / derecha

near / far

cerca / lejos

new / used

nuevo / usado

nothing / something

nada / algo

old / young

viejo / joven

on / off

encendido / apagado

open / closed

abierto / cerrado

quiet / loud

silencioso / ruidoso

rich / poor

rico / pobre

right / wrong

correcto / incorrecto

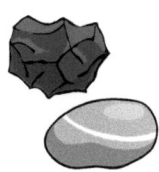

rough / smooth

áspero / suave

sad / happy

triste / contento

short / long

corto / largo

slow / fast

lento / rápido

wet / dry

húmedo / seco

warm / cool

caliente / frío

war / peace

guerra / paz

0

zero

cero

1

one

uno

2

two

dos

3

three

tres

4

four

cuatro

5

five

cinco

6

six

seis

7

seven

siete

8

eight

ocho

9

nine

nueve

10

ten

diez

11

eleven

once

12

twelve

doce

13

thirteen

trece

14

fourteen

catorce

15

fifteen

quince

16

sixteen

dieciséis

17

seventeen

diecisiete

18

eighteen

dieciocho

19

nineteen

diecinueve

20

twenty

veinte

100

hundred

cien

1.000

thousand

mil

1.000.000

million

millón

languages

idiomas

English
....
inglés

American English
....
inglés americano

Chinese Mandarin
....
chino mandarín

Hindi
....
hindi

Spanish
....
español

French
....
francés

Arabic
....
árabe

Russian
....
ruso

Portuguese
....
portugués

Bengali
....
bengalí

German
....
alemán

Japanese
....
japonés

I

yo

you

tú

he / she / it

él / ella

we

nosotros

you

vosotros

they

ellos

who?

¿quién?

what?

¿qué?

how?

¿cómo?

where?

¿dónde?

when?

¿cuándo?

name

nombre

behind

detrás

in

en

in front of

delante de

over

por encima de

on

sobre

under

debajo de

beside

junto a

between

entre

place

lugar

.